"She *must be* Silent"

The Great Commission Bestowed On Both Men & Women

GRACE DOLA BALOGUN

"She *must be* Silent"

"She *must be* Silent"
By Grace Dola Balogun

Copyright ©2013 Grace Dola Balogun

Contact Author at:
www.Gracereligiousbookspublishers.com
1-646-559-2533

Grace Religious Books Publishing & Distributors books may be ordered through booksellers or by contacting the publisher:

Grace Religious Books Publishing & Distributors, Inc.
New York
213 Bennett Avenue
New York, NY 10040

All rights reserved. No part of this book may be used or reproduced by any means, graphic, electronic, or mechanical, including photocopying, recording, taping or by any information storage retrieval system without the written permission of the publisher except in the case of brief quotations embodied in critical articles and reviews.

Because of the dynamic nature of the Internet, any web addresses or links contained in this book may have changed since publication and may no longer be valid. The views expressed in this work are solely those of the author and do not necessarily reflect the views of the publisher, and the publisher hereby disclaims any responsibility for them.

"She *must be* Silent"

The author of this book does not dispense medical advice or prescribe the use of any technique as for treatment for physical, emotional, or medical problems without the advice of a physician, either directly or indirectly. The intent of the author is only to offer information of a general nature to help you in your quest for emotional and spiritual well-being. In the event you use any of the information in this book for yourself, which is your constitutional right, the author and the publisher assume no responsibility for your actions.

Soft Cover: ISBN 9781939415332
Hard Cover: ISBN 9781939415363

Library of Congress Control Number: 2013939774

Editing and Interior Design by CBM Christian Book Marketing
www.christian-book-marketing.com

Cover Design by Lisa Hainline www.lisahainline.com

Printed in the United States of America
Grace Religious Books Publishing & Distributors, Inc. New York

"She *must be* Silent"

"Praise the Lord O my soul, all my inmost being, praise his holy name. Praise the Lord, O my soul, and forget not all his benefits who forgives all your sins and heals all your diseases, who redeems your life from the pit and crowns you with love and compassion, who satisfies your desires with good things so that your youth is renewed like the eagle's."
(Psalm 103: 1-5)

DEDICATION

I dedicate this book to God the Father Almighty who spoke Jesus Christ His begotten Son into being as God's Word and wisdom incarnate. Christ as the attribute of God the Father, just as our words and thoughts come from us and cannot be separated from us, in the same way Jesus Christ cannot be separated from the Father. Christ as the Word of God, the Speech of God, Christ is the living Word of God who lives forevermore. Christ is the wisdom of God and the power of God.

I also dedicate this book to men and women who will read this book and acquire great wisdom and knowledge to believe on the Day of Ascension of our Lord and Savior. He gave The Great Commission to men and women to go and make disciples of all nations without distinction. Also, on the Day of Pentecost, the Spirit of God descended on men and women for the empowerment in the service of the work of the Lord.

"She *must be* Silent"

Women today must see clearly that in Christ the righteousness of God is being revealed from faith to faith. They will live by faith to the point that they will give their lives to the One and only, the Word of God and God. To all the people on Earth that seek after their own wisdom, and finally one day they will come to the knowledge and understanding of the wisdom of God, as well as the authority of the Word of God in their lives.

"She *must be* Silent"

CONTENTS

Dedication 5
Preface 11

CHAPTER ONE 15
THE ROLE OF WOMEN IN THE OLD TESTAMENT

CHAPTER TWO 21
THE ROLE OF PROPHETS AND PROPHETESSES IN THE OLD TESTAMENT

CHAPTER THREE 29
GOD USED MORDECAI AND ESTHER TO SAVE THE JEWISH PEOPLE

CHAPTER FOUR 35
GOD USED ANNA IN THE TEMPLE TO ANNOUNCE THE MESSIAH

CHAPTER FIVE 41
GOD USED HANNAH, MOTHER OF SAMUEL

CHAPTER SIX 47
GOD ACHIEVED HIS PURPOSE THROUGH MOSES' MOTHER

CHAPTER SEVEN 51
HAGAR CALLED ON THE LORD AND HE ANSWERED

CHAPTER EIGHT 55
THE SAMARITAN WOMAN: THE FIRST MISSIONARY

CHAPTER NINE 59
JESUS TAUGHT MARY AND MARTHA ALONG WITH THE APOSTLES

CHAPTER TEN 63
MARY MAGDALENE ANNOUNCED CHRIST'S RESURRECTION

CHAPTER ELEVEN 67
AGUILA AND PRISCILLA TEACH APOLLOS

CHAPTER TWELVE 77
APOSTLE PAUL COMMENDED PHOEBE, A LEADER & PROPHETESS FOR THE SERVICE OF THE LORD

CHAPTER THIRTEEN 83
THE CORINTHIAN CHURCH WOMEN DURING APOSTLE PAUL'S MINISTRY

CHAPTER FOURTEEN 89
WHAT BROUGHT OUT CONFUSION IN THE CORINTH CHURCH?

CHAPTER FIFTEEN 95
CHRIST'S GREAT COMMISSION FOR MEN AND WOMEN BEFORE HIS ASCIENSION

CHAPTER SIXTEEN 101
THE HOLY SPIRIT DECENDED ON THE DAY OF PENTECOST

CHAPTER SEVENTEEN 107
THE HOLY SPIRIT EMPOWERMENT FOR MEN AND WOMEN

CHAPTER EIGHTEEN 113
CHRIST CALLED MEN AND WOMEN TO PREACH, TEACH AND TO THE AUTHORITY OF THE WORD

CHAPTER NINETEEN 117
WOMEN TODAY

CHAPTER TWENY 121
WOMEN ARE EMPOWERED TO PREACH, TEACH AND PRAISE

SUMMARY 125

PRAYER 129

BIBLIOGRAPHY 133

BIBLICAL INDEX 134

ABOUT THE AUTHOR 149

ORDER FORM 151

"She *must be* Silent"

"Praise the Lord. Praise God in his sanctuary, praise him in his mighty heavens. Praise him for his acts of power, praise him for his surpassing greatness. Praise him with the sounding of the trumpet, praise him with the harp and lyre, praise him with tambourine and dancing." (Psalm 150:1-4)

PREFACE

"I do not permit a woman to teach or to have authority over a man, she must be silent."
(1st Timothy 2:12)

Women all over the world see this verse as comprehensively oppressing, declaring permanently and forbidding women not to teach a man. We have to look at another verse where the same Apostle Paul approves the teaching of Priscilla and Aquila teaching, as well as explaining to Apollo the doctrine of Christian baptism.

We also have women teachers and leaders during the time that Paul used this statement in other churches around the world. Priscilla, a woman, did teach Apollo in their house church. Apollo became one of the best preachers of his days in Asia Minor.

"When Priscilla and Aquila heard him, they invited him to their house and explained to him the way of God more adequately" (Acts 18:26). Paul maintained confidence in the abilities of Priscilla and Aquila as both church leaders and he let them lead in their church in Ephesus. This was the church that met together in their house. This should make it clear to women believers that what Paul said was for the Corinthian church alone and not all the existing churches of that time. Paul and Luke did not disapprove of Priscilla teaching Apollo or her role as a leader of the church.

In this writing, believers will see how God used women from the beginning of creation to achieve His purposes. Men and women of God did not possess any authority of their own, rather that authority that came from God. If men and women teach or preach, they are using the authority which God the Father ordained through God the Son.

We have to know as well that many house churches in the early church were hosted and were led by women who were elevated to such a social standard or independently rich, for example: Lydia, Phoebe, Euodia and many others. With this in mind, I urge women of today to give their life to the Lord in faithful and sincere service to the Lord more than ever before in the history of this universe.

"She *must be* Silent"

When men taught or preached, they used the authority of the Word of God. It is the same way when women preached or taught. They also used the authority of the Word of God. It is the same Spirit that indwells both in men and women, using them for the glory of God. Even up until today, this will continue until Christ returns.

"Then the glory of the Lord rose from above the Cherubim and moved to the threshold of the temple. The cloud filled the temple, and the court was full of the radiance of the glory of the Lord." (Ezekiel 10:4)

CHAPTER ONE

THE ROLE OF WOMEN IN THE OLD TESTAMENT

"God created man in his own image, in the image of God he created him; male and female he created them." (Genesis 1:27)

According to the Scripture concerning the creation of human beings, we see clearly and precisely with specific detail, that human beings were created both male and female during creation. This account is very complimentary and teachable, as well as explanatory: both men and women were created in God's own image. We can see that both men and women were a very special creation of God, not a product of evolution. Man and woman were both created in the image and likeness of God.

On the basis of this image, they could respond to and have fellowship with God: "Then God said, let us make man in our image, in our likeness, and let them rule over the fish of the sea and the birds of the air, over the livestock, over all the earth and over all the animals, and over all the creatures that move along the ground" (Genesis 1:26.)

On the basis of this image, they could respond to and have fellowship with God, uniquely reflecting His love, glory, and holiness. Adam and Eve were to do so by knowing God and obeying Him. They possessed a moral likeness to God, for they were sinless and holy, possessing wisdom, a heart of love and the will to do right. They lived in a personal fellowship with God, that which involved moral obedience and intimate communion.

When Adam and Eve sinned, their moral likeness to God was corrupted. In redemption, believers must renew the original moral likeness. Adam and Eve possessed a natural likeness to God. They were created beings with a spirit, mind, emotions, self-consciousness and power of choice. In some sense, man and woman's physical make-up is in God's image in a way that is not true of animals. God gave to human beings the image in which He was to appear visible to them and the form that his Son would one day assume.

Therefore, human beings were made in the image of God. This does not mean they are divine. They have been created in a lower order and are dependent on God. We have to know that all human life is derived initially from Adam and Eve. We need to study this event that according to the attributes and the sovereignty of God, there is no distinction between men and women in the eyes of God.

"Then Miriam, the prophetess, Aaron's sister, took a tambourine in her hand, and all the women followed her, with tambourines and dancing. Sing to the Lord, for he is highly exalted. The horse and its rider he has hurled into the sea." (Exodus 15:21). We read in the Scripture that Prophetess Miriam is called a prophetess because she was highly prophetically gifted by God and she spoke messages from God to the people. In this occasion, she leads the women of Israel in a spontaneous prophetic event. We have to know that in the Old Testament, the characteristic of a prophet or prophetess, must be a person that has a close relationship with God, and became God's confidant. A prophetess is one who sees the world and everything in it, and who also follows the covenant of people from God's perspective, not from a human point of view. Before God could speak through someone, or send a message through someone, the person must have been consecrated and very close to God. A prophetess must love what God loves and hate what God hates. A prophetess must also be sympathetic with God, understanding the dealings by God because of the sin of His people.

"She *must be* Silent"

"Before the mountains were born or you brought forth the earth and the world from everlasting to everlasting you are God." (Psalm 90:2)

"She *must be* Silent"

CHAPTER TWO

THE ROLE OF PROPHETS AND PROPHETESSES IN THE OLD TESTAMENT

A prophetess must, in every way, understand God's prophesy, His will and His desire better than any ordinary people. A prophetess must experience the same emotional reactions God's work in the lives of His people. A prophetess is someone who deeply loves the Lord and His people when they are going through hurt, or pain, or any circumstances or adversities and prays for them.

If God used women prophetesses in the Old Testament in this way, that means God is still calling women to get close to Him today, so that He can put His words in their mouth to preach and teach the Word of God. There is no distinction then, why are we creating distinction that has made women not to serve the Lord today?

"She *must be* Silent"

"Deborah, a prophetess, the wife of Lappidoth, was leading Israel at that time. She held Court under the palm of Deborah between Ramah and Bethel in the hill country of Ephraim, and the Israelites came to her to have their disputes decided. She sent for Barak son of Abinoam from Kedesh in Naphtali and said to him. The Lord God of Israel, commands you: Go, take with you ten thousand men of Naphtali and Zebulon and lead the way to mount Tabor" (Judges 4:4-6).

We read in the Old Testament Scripture how God used Deborah the prophetess with a gift of prophetic message, which enabled her to hear messages from God and communicate God's will to the people. The Prophetess Deborah continues to maintain a close relationship with God who gave her great influence among her people. The same Lord God Almighty, who was yesterday and today in a Kingdom without end, used prophetess Deborah to achieve His purposes in the lives of Israelites. God did not say that Deborah must not use authority or to be silent; God put His Word of authority in Deborah's mouth, and she delivered the message to the people of Israel.

With the Word of God through Deborah, the prophetess, God went before the Israelites and achieved a great thing. It is very essential that God goes before us to prepare the way, unless He guides us along the way, our endeavors and our labors will fail. Consequently, we must earnestly seek to be open to God's continual leading in our lives.

Moses cried to God in the wilderness, "Then Moses said to him, if your presence does not go with us, do not send us up from here" (Exodus 33:15). All God's people must know and pray fervently without ceasing to know God's way for their lives in addition to know God's heart, His purposes, His wisdom, His holy principles, and even His suffering so much that they come to know God Himself and hear His words spoken to their heart. Then, in this, His will be done in their lives.

The Scripture also mentioned how men and women work together: "The whole company numbered 42,307 besides their 7,337 men servants and maid servants; and they also had 200 men and women singers" (Ezra 2:64-65). All these people mentioned here in the Book of Ezra, both men and women, including the singers, work together for the glory of God.

There was no mention of anyone using authority over another. This shows clearly that God is the one and only that gives orders and controls through His created beings as men and women. He commanded and created.

"She *must be* Silent"

He is the same God of yesterday, today, and forever in a Kingdom without end. The Scripture also stated clearly how God used the Prophetess Huldah, a messenger of the Lord, "Hilkiah and those the King had sent with him went to speak to the prophetess Huldah, who was the wife of Shallum son of Tokhath the Son of Hasrah, keeper of the wardrobe. (She lived in Jerusalem, in the second district.) She said to them, "This is what the Lord, the God of Israel, says, "Tell the man who sent you to me, this is what the Lord says, "I am going to bring disaster on this place and its people - all curses written in the book that has been read in the presence of the King of Judah, because they have forsaken me, and burned incense to other gods and provoked me to anger by all that their hands have made, my anger will be poured out on this place and will not be quenched. Tell the King of Judah, who sent you to inquire of the Lord, this is what the Lord, the God of Israel, says concerning the words you heard" (2nd Chronicles 34:22-26).

In this case God used another prophetess called Huldah to deliver His message because the sins of the people of Israel had reached to such a point that God's destructive judgment on the people was inevitable. We see that prophetess Huldah humbled herself, she got close to the Lord up to the point that Hilkiah, the priest, sent people to her to find what God's purpose is for them. If we, as men and women, would humble ourselves before the Lord God, this is the primary condition for God to use us, renew us and then we are able to receive God's grace.

"And afterwards, I will pour out my Spirit on all people: your sons and daughters will prophesy your old men will dream dreams; your young men will see visions Even on my servants, both men and women, I will pour out my Spirit in those days" (Joel 2:28-29). Prophet Joel predicts that a day will come that God will pour out His Spirit on both men and women, as well as on everyone who calls on the name of the Lord.

This out pouring will result in a charismatic show of the Spirit and the prophetic manifestation among God's people throughout the world. This prophetic message was fulfilled on the day of Pentecost, when the Spirit of the Lord descended from Heaven like a rushing wind and manifested upon men and women. Apostle Peter quoted this verse from the Book of Joel on the Day of Pentecost. He explained that the outpouring of the Spirit on that day was the beginning of the fulfillment of Joel's prophesies. This promise has been ongoing unto those and all who accept Jesus Christ as their Lord and Savior because all the believers must be filled with the Holy Spirit. Your sons and daughters will prophesy, Joel envisions that one of the primary results of the outpouring of the Holy Spirit will be the impartation and the release of prophetic gifts of the Holy Spirit.

The manifestation of the Holy Spirit through His gifts makes known God's presence among His people. A review of this prophesy shows that was fulfilled on the day of Pentecost therefore exhibits that both men and women are called to serve the Lord in singleness of heart and in the Spirit of holiness.

The Spirit was not poured on men alone; it was out pouring at the same time on both men and women. Both have the power to teach, preach and take the Gospel to the end of the Earth just as men did for the glory of our Lord and Savior Jesus Christ.

"She *must be* Silent"

"Many, O Lord my God, are the wonders you have done. The things you planned for us no one can recount to you; were I to speak and tell of them, they would be too many to declare." (Psalm 40:5)

"She *must be* Silent"

CHAPTER THREE

GOD USED MORDECAI AND ESTHER TO SAVE THE JEWISH PEOPLE

"For if you remain silent at this time, relief and deliverance for the Jews will arise from another place, but you and your father's family will perish. And who knows but that you have come to royal position for such a time as this?"(Esther 4:14)

Esther is one of the great women in the Old Testament that the Lord moves up to a position of queen in order to use her to save the Israelites, through Mordecai that was a man of God.

We see that God used both of them to achieve His purpose in a deadly situation and plot. A man called Haman was the prime minister of Persia. He was the first political person in the Scripture to devise a plan for the exterminating all the Jews within his political sphere. Haman plot of genocide against the Jewish people has its parallel in Antiochus Epiphanies' plot in the second century.

Haman used something similar to dice. Haman used it to determine the lucky day on which he would destroy the Jews. He determined that within one year intervals, the casting lot and the execution of the plan will be accomplished, this gave Mordecai and Ester, under God's providence time to cancel Haman's evil plot. One of God's purposes in giving the law to Israel was to make them different from all other people on Earth. Haman recognized something different in the Jews and hated them for it.

Under the New Covenant, God still wants His people to be separated and different from the world. Likewise today, the world, still hates God's people because they are different, holy and righteous and because they are children of God.

Mordecai believed that it was God's purpose to use Esther to deliver Israel and that she had become the Queen for this very reason. However, Mordecai knew that Esther could fall short of that purpose if she did not do her part in God's redemptive plan. If she refused to help the Jews, she too would perish. God's sovereign purposes usually includes human responsibility. We have to see clearly that God is always involved in the events of the world in order to save His people from this evil and to accomplish His redemptive purposes on their behalf. All believers must remember that God is working in what happens around believers, in order to rescue them from this present evil age and to bring believers to live with Him forever.

Esther was willing to give her life in an attempt to save her people. Esther decided and was ready to do what was right and leave the consequences in the hands of God. God will not honor those who remain silent in order to protect their place in the church, or in the society, and He will not honor those who remain silent in order to protect their position, but he will honor those who, for the sake of God and His word, speak the truth in the face of great danger. Mordecai and Esther were willing to be, if need be, in their efforts against a plot of evil.

Mordecai and Esther can be seen as an example of the great people of faith and integrity who do not compromise their conscience or bend under the pressure of evil intimidation. They are ready to serve the Lord and they are ready to take the Gospel to the end of the Earth for Christ. They said that they don't care if they perish as long as Christ is preaching and the Gospel of God reaches the ends of the Earth; therefore, they will rejoice. We have to give thanks to the Lord that He is still doing His work through believers, achieving His purposes through believers and making disciples of all nations. Through men and women people are being saved, the Gospel is being taught and preached. Thanks be to Jesus Christ through the power of indwelling of the Holy Spirit.

"She *must be* Silent"

"Sacrifice and offering you did not desire, but my ears you have pierced, burnt offerings and sin offerings you did not require." (Psalm 40:6)

"She *must be* Silent"

CHAPTER FOUR

GOD USED SIMEON AND ANNA IN THE TEMPLE TO ANNOUNCE THE MESSIAH

"On the eighth day, when it was time to circumcise him, he was named Jesus, the name the angel had given him before he had been conceived. When the time of their purification according to the Law of Moses had been completed, Joseph and Mary took him to Jerusalem to present him to the Lord as it is written in the Law of the Lord. Every firstborn male is to be consecrated to the Lord, and to offer a sacrifice in keeping with what is said in the Law of the Lord, a pair of doves or two young pigeons. Now there was a man in Jerusalem called Simeon, who was righteous and devout. He was waiting for the consolation of Israel, and the Holy Spirit was upon him. It had been revealed to him by the Holy Spirit that he would not die before he had seen the

Lord's Christ. Moved by the spirit, he went into the temple courts. When the parents brought the child Jesus to do for him what the custom of the Law required. Simeon took him in his arms and praised God" (Luke 2:21-28).

According to the Scripture, "There was also a prophetess, Anna the Daughter of Phanuel, of the tribe of Asher. She was very old; she had lived with her husband seven years after her marriage, and then was a widow until she was eighty-four. She never left the temple but worshiped night and day, fasting and praying. Coming up to them at that very moment, she gave thanks to God and spoke about the child to all who were looking forward to the redemption of Jerusalem" (Luke 2:36-38).

Anna was a prophetess who earnestly hoped for the coming of Christ. She remained a widow for many years, never remarrying, but devoting herself to the Lord with fasting and praying, night and day. God used Anna, a prophetess in the Temple, for many years and God gave her assurance that she would still be alive when the Messiah would be born. The Bible teaches that, "An unmarried man and woman is concerned about the Lord's affairs, how he can please the Lord. But married men and women are concerned about the affairs of this world, how he can please his wife or husband (1st Corinthians 7:32-33).

"She *must be* Silent"

Unmarried people can be a greater blessing than the married individuals. Anna gave testimony when Jesus Christ the Messiah was brought to the Temple for purification. Simeon and Anna were both righteous and devout; they were upright in the eyes of the Lord. They were right with God in heart and in action, righteousness that God sought in the Old Testament was one that came from the heart, based on true faith, in love and with the fear of God. This condition of the heart was seen in the parents of John the Baptist, who observed all the Lord's commandments and regulations blamelessly. Both Simeon and Anna manifested the same characteristic in their lives.

As Joseph and Mary presented Jesus to the Lord, so all parents should sincerely consecrate their children to the Lord. They should also pray constantly that from the beginning to the end of each child's life, he or she will be found doing the will of the Lord, serving and glorifying God with complete devotion.

God is still using men and women in this current day. Anna was a prophetess who works in the Temple day and night praying for the coming of the Messiah. She gets close to and consecrated her life to the Lord, devoting herself to God by fasting and praying day and night. Because of Anna's devotion and dedication to the Lord, she was there in the Temple when they brought Jesus for purification. We have to thank God for revealing His prophetic word, His Will and purposes to men and women from the Old Testament to New Testament.

"She *must be* Silent"

"Then I said, "Here I am, I have come -- it is written about me in the scroll. I desire to do your will, O my God; your law is within my heart." (Psalm 40:7-8)

"She *must be* Silent"

CHAPTER FIVE

GOD USED HANNAH, MOTHER OF SAMUEL

The Old Testament prophets were men and women of God who leaned toward the spiritual over contemporary concerns. There are no other categories of people in the Scriptures that present the dramatic picture of God's revelations than the Old Testament prophets and prophetesses, priests, judges, kings, wise counselors and the psalmists. Prophets and prophetesses prophesy as to what God puts in their mouth, abundantly from God's mind and by God's Spirit. They are the messengers, or spoke persons for the Lord who poured out words of God under the indwelling power of the Spirit of God. Prophets and prophetesses are the one who speak on behalf of God; they are the spokesmen for God and they are servants of God. God gave them His Spirit for that purpose and after, he took away the Spirit until He

"She *must be* Silent"

wanted them to speak for Him again. They called them in the Old Testament the man who has the Spirit of God in him.

They are not just another religious leader, but one into whom God's Spirit and God's word had entered and taken possession because the Spirit and the Word of God were in him. The Old Testament prophet and prophetess had three characteristics, which are: (a) divinely revealed knowledge, which they experience God given knowledge with respect to events, people, and redemptive truth. The primary purpose of the prophets and prophetesses is to encourage God's people to remain faithful to God's covenant to make God's will clear to the people by way of instruction, correction and warnings from God. Most importantly, God used the prophets and prophetess to pronounce His judgment before it happened. God revealed to them about the coming of the Messiah, as well as other future predictions. God, in His mercy and love, continue to do the same today. (b) God divinely gives powers to prophets and prophetesses as they were drawn into the sphere of the miraculous as they were filled with the Spirit of God. Through God's prophets and prophetesses lives the power of God in that they were able to demonstrate in supernatural ways to the world of sin. (c) God created

"She *must be* Silent"

distinctive lifestyles for his prophets and prophetesses by abandoning old way of life and living exclusively for God. Prophets and prophetesses protested rigorously against idolatry, immorality, and all evils that filled the world. They work hard to bring the holiness of God to the people. With this in mind, we have to know that God continues to use men and women to serve Him up until today.

"Once when they had finished eating and drinking in Shiloh, Hannah stood up. Now Eli the Priest was sitting on a chair by the doorpost of the Lord's temple. In bitterness of soul Hannah wept much and prayed to the Lord. And she made a vow, saying, 'O Lord Almighty, if you will only look upon your servant's misery and remember me and not forget your servant but give her a son, then I will give him to the Lord for all the days of his life, and no razor will ever be used on his head' " (1st Samuel 1:9-11). We can see the hand of God in Hannah's life. Her barrenness is ascribed directly to the activity of God. He is the one and only doing and undoing in our lives. God had withheld children in order to prepare her for the birth of her son, Samuel, who would become a great prophet of the Lord. Hannah's experience of barrenness, frustration, shame and waiting was a trial of her faith. But the desperate intercession produced in her prepared the way of a miracle of God to come forth and for God's prophetic plan to be manifested. In the same way today, at times, God may cause us to experience disappointment, spiritual barrenness and brokenness so that we cry out in desperation to God for His holy intervention. We believers today, especially women should copy Hannah by taking our unbearable situations and pain directly to the Lord and wait for Him to answer.

Hannah showed her gratitude to the Lord. She also showed her unwavering love and devotion to God by her promise of willingness to dedicate her son to the Lord's work In the same way today Christian parents may express their commitment to God and His Kingdom by giving their sons and daughters to the ministry work of missions in other lands.

Those parents, who support, encourage and pray for their children will find great favor with God. God used Hannah to bring Samuel, the great prophet of the Lord to the world, which also brought great change to the people of Israel. God still uses women today to birth many miraculous things.

"She *must be* Silent"

"I proclaim righteousness in the great assembly; I do not seal my lips, as you know, O Lord. I do not hide your righteousness in my heart I speak of your faithfulness and salvation." (Psalm 40:9-10)

"She *must be* Silent"

CHAPTER SIX

GOD ACHIEVED HIS PURPOSE THROUGH MOSES' MOTHER

"Now a man of the house of Levi married a Levite woman and she became pregnant and gave birth to a son. When she saw that he was a fine child, she hid him for three months. But when she could hide him no longer, she got a papyrus basket for him and coated it with tar and pitch. Then she placed the child in it and put it among the reeds along the bank of Nile. His sister stood at a distance to see what would happen to him. Then Pharaoh's daughter went down to the Nile to bathe, and her attendants were walking along the riverbank. She saw the basket among the reeds and sent her slave girl to get it. She opened it and saw the baby. He was crying, and she felt sorry for him. This is one of the Hebrews babies, she said. Then his sister asked Pharaoh's daughter, 'Shall I go and get one of the Hebrew women to nurse the baby for you?' 'Yes, go,' she answered. And the girl went and got the baby's mother. Pharaoh's daughter said to her, 'Take this baby and nurse him for me, and I will pay you.' So the woman took the baby and nursed him. When the child grew older, she took him to Pharaoh's daughter and he became her son. She named him Moses, saying, "I drew him out of the water" (Exodus 2:1-10).

    We can see that God used Moses' mother, Moses' sister, Pharaoh Daughter's attendant and Pharaoh's daughter to achieve His purpose for the children of Israel to bring freedom from slavery. Moses' birth, all the plans of his mother in order to escape from death, and all the events of his youth were all under God's divine direction in order that he might deliver the people of Israel from the bondage of slavery.

    This is the same God that all believers need to know that God also works in their lives, using the right means and tools to accomplish His divine will. God is the orchestrator and He is the author and finisher of our faith.

"She *must be* Silent"

"I do not conceal your love and your truth from the great assemble. Do not withhold your mercy from me, O Lord; may your love and your truth always protect me."
(Psalm 40: 10b-11)

"She *must be* Silent"

CHAPTER SEVEN

HAGAR CALLED ON THE LORD AND HE ANSWERED

God used Hagar, mother of Ishmael, to bless all the descendants of Ishmael. "Early the next morning Abraham took some food and a skin of water and gave them to Hagar. He set them on her shoulders and then set her off with the boy. She went in her way and wandered in the desert of Beersheba. When the water in the skin was gone. She put the boy under one of the bushes. Then she went off and sat down nearby, about a bowshot away. She thought, "I cannot watch the boy die. And as she sat there nearby she began to sob. God heard the boy crying and the angel of God called to Hagar from heaven and said to her, 'what is the matter, Hagar? Do not be afraid; God has heard the boy's crying as he lies there. Lift the boy up and take him by the hand, for I will make him a great nation. Then opened her eyes and she saw a well of water. So she went and filled the skin with water and gave the boy a drink" (Genesis 21:14-19).

God heard the cry of the boy. Because the boy was innocent in the middle of what took place before he was conceived and born to this Earth. God knew it was best that Hagar and Ishmael leave Abraham's house in that he can test Abraham and also make Ishmael strong. Nevertheless, God did not forsake Hagar and Ishmael, for they remained in His presence and under His care.

God always had a purpose for Ishmael that parallels His purpose for Isaac. God promised that He would make Ishmael into a great nation. God is always concerned about the welfare of men and women today and forever; He always exercises His mercy and enduring loving kindness in our lives.

"She *must be* Silent"

"For troubles without number surround me; my sins have overtaken me, and I cannot see. They are more than the hairs of my head, and my heart fails within me."
(Psalm 40:12)

"She *must be* Silent"

CHAPTER EIGHT

THE SAMARITAN WOMAN: THE FIRST MISSIONARY

"When a Samaritan woman came to draw water, Jesus said to her, 'Will you give me a drink?' His disciples had gone into the town to buy food. The Samaritan woman said to him, 'You are a Jew and I am a Samaritan woman. How can you ask me for a drink' " (John 4:7-9)?. Jesus later: "Go call your husband and come back" (John 4:16). "Then, leaving her water jar, the woman went back to the town and said to the people. 'Come; see a man who told me everything I ever did. Could this be Christ?' They came out of the town and made their way towards him" (John 4:28-30). So when the Samaritans came to him, they urged him to stay with them, and he stayed two days. And because of his words many more became believers. They said, to the woman, we no longer believe just because of

"She *must be* Silent"

what you said, now we have heard for ourselves, and we know that this man really is the Savior of the world" (John 4:39-42). The Samaritan woman was the first to take the Gospel to the people of her village. Jesus Christ told her to go and call her husband, but she told him she does not have one, but with her love for the truth of the word of God that she received from Jesus, she was very happy to tell all the people in her village that Jesus is the Christ, the Messiah that was supposed to come to deliver His people. The people of the village first received the word from the woman, and the Holy Spirit through Christ expounded it, imparted it to their hearts making them believers and assured them that this is Christ, the expected Messiah.

Today, we must take the Gospel to people in our family, on our jobs and in our schools. We must try our best to share the love of God with all the people in the world. Also when we give the Word of God to the people, the Word of God is God whether or not it came from a man or woman, it is the same the word of God.

The Holy Spirit is the one that will use it to touch the hearts, minds, souls and spirits. Telling women not to teach and preach is not what Christ said. Both men and women were told and they were saved in the village. We believers we are to sow the seed Jesus Christ is the one that increases it and makes it grow in the hearts and minds of the people.

Women are equal and qualified to preach, teach and proclaim the Gospel of God, just as men, because the Spirit of God was poured on both men and women on the same date at the same time on the day of Pentecost. Those who bring others to saving faith in Jesus Christ are doing something of eternal consequence. They will one day rejoice in Heaven over those who were saved because of their prayers and their witnesses. At the same time, believers must understand that their work and services is often a reaping of the labors of others.

The entire fruitful ministry we have for God is in a large part as a result of the sacrificial labor of the redemptive work of Christ and collective works and services of all believers in Heaven and on Earth.

"She *must be* Silent"

Be pleased, O Lord, to save me; O Lord, come quickly to help me. May all who seek to take my life, be put to shame and confusion; may all who desire my ruin be turned back in disgrace. "Aha! Aha!" be appalled at their own shame."

(Psalm 40:13-15)

CHAPTER NINE

JESUS TAUGHT MARY AND MARTHA ALONG WITH THE APOSTLES

"As Jesus and his disciples were on their way, he came to a village where a woman named Martha opened her home to him. She had a sister called Mary, who sat at the Lord's feet listening to what he said. But Martha was distracted by all the preparations that had to be made. She came to him and asked, 'Lord, don't you care that my sister has left me to do the work by myself? Tell her to help me!' 'Martha, Martha, the Lord answered, you are worried and upset about many things, but only one thing is needed. Mary has chosen what is better, and it will not be taken away from her" (Luke 10:38-42). We can see in this scripture clearly that Mary was sitting with our Lord Jesus Christ during one of His teachings during His earthly ministry. Mary was not the only female at the feet of Christ learning about the Kingdom of God. Jesus Christ did not tell her to go and cook with her sister because she was a woman.

Jesus Christ said that Mary has chosen what is better, which her salvation and the teaching of the Word of God that can never be erased from her memory. What is needed on the Earth is to be active in the practical service of God, which is very essential and good. We have to make ourselves available in the service of God. Our first and most important task is our love and devotion that will express itself in a quiet worship, prayer and fellowship with the Lord at all times.

Believers must not be so busy doing the work of the Lord, attending all church services and performing good deeds that they forget the first and greatest duty which is to love for the Lord God himself with all their hearts, souls, strength and minds. Both men and women should care to offer themselves a living sacrifice in the work of the Lord. Although when He called, He called the disciples that were all men because men at that time were the ones that were going to school during or learning under the Rabbi, such as Gamaliel, but today some women have more education than men. We should use our knowledge of education to serve the Lord.

"She *must be* Silent"

"But may all who seek you rejoice and be glad in you; may those who love your salvation always say, "The Lord, be exalted! Yet I am poor and needy; may the Lord think of me. You are my help and my deliverer; O my God, do not delay." (Psalm 40: 16-17)

"She *must be* Silent"

CHAPTER TEN

MARY MAGDALENE ANNOUNCED CHRIST'S RESURRECTION

"Jesus said do not hold on to me, for I have not yet returned to the Father. Go instead to my brothers and tell them, I am returning to my Father and your Father, to my God and your God." (John 20:17)

We see in this case, after the resurrection of Jesus Christ, that He appeared to Mary. The first person to whom Jesus appears after His resurrection is Mary. Mary is a woman; our Lord did not say, "Yes, Mary is a woman. I will not appear to her." With this illustration and opening up of Scripture you will that Jesus Christ wants women to serve Him by taking the Gospel to the end of the world.

Mary is not a prominent or a particular person in the gospels, yet Jesus Christ, our Savior and Lord, appears first

"She *must be* Silent"

to her, rather than any of the outstanding leaders among the disciples. Throughout the ages Jesus Christ always call ordinary people to serve Him. Jesus reveals His presence and love especially to those who are nobody, or least. God's special people are the unknown, those who, like Mary in her grief, maintained a steadfast love for the Lord.

The Lord will reveal Himself to those who love Him and gave their life to Him. He sent Mary to the disciples and He did not wait until He saw any of the men. This will let you know men and women are equal in the hands of our Lord; there is no distinction. It is the same spirit of Jesus baptizing all the believers - men and women. Women must not be silent in the church; they must be very active, praying without ceasing teaches everyone and witnesses to both men and women on the street and in the church. Women should work hard in the service of the Lord in order to bring glory to His Holy name.

"She *must be* Silent"

Trust in the Lord and do good; dwell in the land and enjoy safe pasture. Delight yourself in the Lord and he will give you the desires of your heart. Commit your way to the Lord; trust in him and he will do this; He will make your righteousness shine like the dawn, the justice of your cause like the noonday sun."(Psalm 37:3-6)

"She *must be* Silent"

CHAPTER ELEVEN

AGUILA AND PRISCILLA TEACH APOLLOS

"Paul stayed on in Corinth for some time, and then he left the brothers and sailed for Syria accompanied by Priscilla and Aguila. Meanwhile, a Jew named Apollos, a native of Alexandria, came to Ephesus. He was a learned man, with a thorough knowledge of the Scriptures. He had been instructed in the way of the Lord, and he spoke with great fervor and taught about Jesus accurately, though he knew only the baptism of John. He began to speak boldly in the synagogue. When Priscilla and Aguila heard him, they invited him to their home and explained to him the way of God more adequately" (Acts 18:18, 24-26). The Scripture is telling is here that both Priscilla and her husband Aguila taught Apollos about the New Testament, the Holy Spirit and the baptism of the Holy Spirit. They explained to Apollos thoroughly and more adequately about the love of God and the power of God, which is in Christ Jesus that is different from baptism of John to repentance. We women believers should copy this and should not stop in our efforts in teaching and preaching, witnessing of the Gospel of God. After the teaching of Priscilla and Aguila, Apollos' understanding of the Gospel was double. Compared to John's baptism, he believed in Jesus as the crucified and resurrected Messiah. Apollos did not learn that Jesus himself was the one baptism for all his believers in the Holy Spirit.

Nothing should hold women back from preaching, teaching or witnessing or engaging in the services of the Lord in this world. We are all in Christ and we are to live with Him and to be useful to Him, doing our best in everything we do in order to bring glory to His Holy name.

Only one biblical Scripture says a woman must not teach a man: "I do not permit a woman to teach or to have authority over a man; she must be silent" (1st Corinthians 2:12). Some churches or Christian organizations used this verse to universally stop every woman Christian from teaching any man, or preaching the Gospel. They used it as an advantage to oppress women in the entire world. They used this verse, which was just a mere word of Paul not the Spirit order, or from the Lord to put down women in the work and services of the Lord. But the same Paul in the Book of Romans commended Phoebe and in the Book of Acts, " He began to speak boldly in the synagogue. When Priscilla and Aguila heard him, they invited him to their home and explained to him the way of God more adequately" (Acts 18:26). This verse sheds a light to what Paul said in the Book of Timothy. This biblical truth where Priscilla a woman of God, with her husband Aguila, teaches and analyzed clearly the ministry of baptism to Apollos, a new convert.

People should read this verse and understand that what Paul said in 1st Timothy is not biblical to the Christian doctrine. Christ called men and women to serve Him. Moreover, we are New Testament believers, whatever Adam and Eve did should not concern us because Jesus Christ has washed away Adam & Eve's sin from believers. We are not in Adam; we are in Christ. Christ paid it all, and we have faith in Christ, we give our life to Christ, not to Adam and Eve.

We are in Christ and Christ in us the hope of glory. I pray that this book will be read by all the women in the world. I pray that Jesus Christ will use this book to lift up women from the bondage of oppression of every church that does not want women to teach or preach or use authority of the Word of God on men. There is no authority for individuals in Christ; Jesus is our authority. Believers have no authority. "Then Jesus came to them and said, "All authority in heaven and on earth has been given to me. Therefore go and make disciples of all nations, baptizing them in the name of the Father and of the son and of the Holy Spirit, and teaching them to obey everything I have commanded you. And surely I am with you always to the very end of the age" (Matthew 28:18-20). All authority belongs to Jesus Christ, authority has been given to Him in heaven and on this Earth and the indwelling of the Holy Spirit uses Christ's authority through all the believers, both men and women, with no exception. He put His Word of authority in the mouth and on the lips of every Christian when He gave them the Great Commission. Therefore, whether you are a man or a woman, the authority of the Word of God is what you are teaching or preaching, not your word. No one has authority of their own.

The authority that exists is the authority of the Word of God to proclaim the Gospel of God. Priscilla is one of the leaders of the local church. Priscilla and Aguila invited Apollos to their home where they explained to him the Christian faith and the doctrine of baptism; both husband and wife took this as their responsibility to teach

"She *must be* Silent"

Apollos. The fact that Priscilla's name was mentioned first according to the early church methods means that she was more active and more involved than her husband. Consequently, we must know that explaining is the same as communicating and communicating includes teaching and instruction, which means to provide instruction whether formal or informal, in writing, orally or physically. Apollos understanding of the Gospel of God was limited. He had accepted John's baptism and believed in Jesus Christ as the crucified and resurrected Messiah. What he had not learned and lacked was that Jesus himself was baptizing all believers in the Holy Spirit. We can see that Paul referring back to Adam's sin means that he was teaching the Old Testament with the New Testament and that is one of the reasons why he put women down in the Book of Timothy.

Priscilla and Aguila heard Apollos preaching in the synagogue; they then expounded to him the way of God more perfectly. They encouraged him in his ministry by diligently and constantly attending wherever he preached. It is the same today with our young ministers that are hopeful. They must be acquainted to the elderly Christians, either men or women. Priscilla and her husband communicated what they knew to Apollos and gave him a

"She *must be* Silent"

clear methodical account of those things, which before he had been confused about, that was made clear to him through their instruction.

Priscilla, with her husband Aguila, teach Apollos. As church leaders, there was many occasions where Priscilla and her husband taught, either formally or informally or during the church meetings.

The Scripture says that Apostle Paul, "Paul wanted to take Timothy along on the journey, so he circumcised him because of the Jews who lived in that area" (Acts 16:3). We also read in the Book of Galatians that says Paul opposes Peter. "When Peter came to Antioch, I opposed him to his face, because he was clearly in the wrong. Before certain men came from James, he used to eat with the Gentiles. But when they arrived, he began to draw back and separate himself from the Gentiles because he was afraid of those who belonged to the circumcision group. The other Jews joined him in his hypocrisy, so that by their hypocrisy even Barnabas was led astray. When I saw that they were not acting in line with the truth of the gospel, I said to Peter in front of them all. You are a Jew, yet you live like a Gentile and not like a Jew. How is it, then, that you force Gentiles to follow Jewish customs?" (Galatians 2: 11-14).

"She *must be* Silent"

The same Apostle Paul was opposed to any spiritual leader who is guilty of error, in this case hypocrisy and ethnic discrimination, must be opposed and rebuked. This must be applied without respect of persons; even a prominent person like the Apostle Peter, who was used mightily by God, needed in this instance corrective rebuke. Scripture indicates that Peter recognized his error and accepted Paul's rebuke in a humble and repentant manner. We should not go back to circumcision, which is the Old Testament sign for the Jewish. The same Paul that went back to the Old Testament sign and circumcised Timothy, rebuked Peter for going back to the Old Testament by not wanting to eat with the Gentiles. We read clearly here that Paul went back to the Old Testament by circumcising Timothy. The same Paul also according to the Scripture, there was no written document that says Paul disapproved Aguila and Priscilla's teaching or her role as a leader of the church concerning Apollos or anyone else in the Scripture. In the Christian light of this the ban, or instruction of Apostle Paul telling women not to teach, while in the book women were teaching should be overlooked and seen as the word of Paul, not from the Spirit of God.

I pray that this verse of the Scripture that causes confusion and relegated women down in the work of the

Lord must be overlooked and men and women must continue serving the Lord faithfully until He returns and sets up His Kingdom. He will straighten everything out for believers; we are all children of God; we must serve Him with the Spirit of holiness.

"She *must be* Silent"

"The Lord is my light and my salvation whom shall I fear? The Lord is the stronghold of my life of whom shall I be afraid? When evil men advance against me to devour my flesh, when my enemies and my foes attack me, they will stumble and fall." (Psalm 27: 1-2)

"She *must be* Silent"

"She *must be* Silent"

CHAPTER TWELVE

THE CORINTHIAN CHURCH WOMEN DURING APOSTLE PAUL'S MINISTRY

"Two or three prophets should speak, and the others should weigh carefully what is said. And if a revelation comes to someone who is sitting down, the first speaker should stop. For you can all prophesy in turn so that everyone may be instructed and encouraged." (1st Corinthians 14:29-31)

From this verse of the Scripture we can easily know that there were so many arguments going on in the Corinthian church between the congregation that consisted both of men and women. Everyone waited to prophesy, even if they were not anointed to do so, as Paul was telling them that all prophesy must be evaluated to know if it is what it said, they believed that the New

Testament prophesy was less than infallible and might need to be corrected. They believed that prophecy and the speaking in tongues might not be a word from God. It could be from an evil spirit or hindering spirit because of the false teachers or false prophets.

During that time, many women wanted to be a prophetess and spoke in tongues, which is still going on today in some churches around the nations. It gets to the point that prophesying, speaking in tongues or possessing any supernatural gift is no guarantee one is a true prophet, or a true believer. Even today, some of the believers' spiritual gifts may be counterfeited by Satan. The church must set up a proper and orderly way to judge prophecies; otherwise, it will fail to follow the biblical guidelines.

The church decided that all prophecy must be tested according to the standard of biblical truth. Many people do not want to agree to these rules, especially women; therefore, Apostle Paul, came up with an order, believing that if he got the women out of the picture, he would be able to control men in the church, and if women wanted to know anything they should ask their husband at home. Scriptures states, "As in all the congregations of the saint, women should remain silent in the churches. They are not allowed to speak, but must be in submission, as the Law says. If they want to inquire about something, they should ask their own husband at home; for it is disgraceful for a woman to speak in the church" (1st Corinthians 14:33-35). We have to notice the sentence here that Apostle Paul said that as in the Law, he did not said that what he was saying was from the Lord, he was giving order to those women who were making or creating problems in the church by claiming certain spiritual power, and speaking in tongues without anyone interpreting what they were speaking to the church.

One of the surest signs that the Holy Spirit is present and at work in any congregation is his conviction of sin, righteousness and judgment. Through the manifestation of the Holy Spirit among God's people, sin will be exposed, repentance called for and sinners convicted. The principal purpose of all spiritual gifts is to strengthen the church and the individual, to promote spiritual life of believers in maturity and good behavioral character in all the believers.

If this is not happening, the person is not yet converted. There must be an order in the church. Paul said he forbade women not to interrupt the service by asking questions that could be asked at home. It is the same way today, some women still talk in the church and they still feel that they are better or more spiritual than other women in the church. But the point is that what Paul said was just to discipline women in the Corinthian church, not in all the churches.

The early church picked it up and turned it upside down to oppress women for many years. Unfortunately, today some churches will not allow women to preach, teach or witness to men, although women are still in the choir, and among the praise and worship teams. Women are still working in the children Bible study classes and within the children music choir. What we need to know is that women cannot do without serving the Lord. We rarely have men in the church. Today women are 98% to one man in some churches all around the world.

One thing we need to notice is how many times our Lord Jesus Christ during his earthly ministry rebuked Apostle Peter for saying wrong things such as: "From that time on Jesus began to explain to his disciples that he must go to Jerusalem and suffer many things at the hands of the elders, chief priest and teachers of the law, and that he must be killed and on the third day be raised to life. Peter took him aside and began to rebuke him. 'Never, Lord,' he said. 'This shall never happen to you' Jesus turned and said to Peter, 'Get behind me, Satan. You are a stumbling block to

"She *must be* Silent"

me; you do not have in mind the things of God, but the things of men' " (Matthew 16:21-23). Our Lord rebuked Peter, but he did not relegate him down. At the end, Peter was the one Jesus spoke to before His ascension to feed His sheep, or to take care of the flocks. Therefore, why is it that Apostle Paul used that sentence to discipline women in the Corinthian church and the men of those days turned it against all the generations of women in the world? Jesus Christ is the author and finisher of our faith. We as believers must move on in the perfection of serving our Lord and Savior Jesus Christ who called both men and women to serve Him.

"She *must be* Silent"

"Though an army besiege me, my heart will not fear, though war break out against me, even then will I be confident." (Psalm 27:3)

CHAPTER THIRTEEN

APOSTLE PAUL COMMENDED PHOEBE A LEADER & PROPHETESS FOR THE SERVICE OF THE LORD

"I commend to you our sister Phoebe a servant of the church in Cenchrea. I ask you to receive her in the Lord in a way worthy of the saints and to give her any help she may need from you, for she has been a great help to many people, including me" (Romans 16:1-2). Phoebe was rich and wealthy; she served the church out of her resources just as some women served Jesus during his earthly ministry.

Phoebe was probably the one who delivered this letter to the Romans. She was a servant - a woman, a Deacon in the church at Cenchrea who ministered to the poor, the sick and the needy, as well as assisted the missionaries such as Paul. Paul's greetings to no less than eight women in this chapter indicate that women performed distinguished service in the churches. Phoebe was a person of quality and estate, who had a business which made her travel to Rome, where she was a stranger and therefore, Paul recommends her to the Christians in Rome. Both Christ and His apostles had some of their best friends among devout women.

"There is no authority except from God, and those authorities that exist have been instituted by God" (Romans 13:1.) "Everyone must submit himself to the governing authority, for there is no authority except that which God has established. The authorities that exist have been established by God. Consequently, he who rebels against the authority is rebelling against what God has instituted, and those who do so will bring judgment on themselves" (Roman 13:1-2).

God commands Christians to obey the state, for the state as an institution is ordained and established by God. God has instituted the government because in this fallen world we need certain restraints to protect us from the chaos and lawlessness that is a natural result of sin.

Many women have been ordained by God to do miraculous works that no man can do. Phoebe was a hard working Deacon and female leader in her church. She was designated as Deacon in the Scripture. Phoebe represents one of the ways in the history of the church how authority was exercised in the life of the church during the early church where believers in Jesus Christ confessed that Jesus Christ is the source of authority as their Lord and Savior.

In the life of Paul's ministry and Phoebe, the power of the Holy Spirit have been exercised. The Spirit of God used both of them as He pleased. Phoebe traveled to Rome all the time on business trips, Paul used her to carry the letters of the church back and forth, which Paul was greatly appreciated. This is Paul that says women should be silent in the church at Corinth. Phoebe is remembered by Paul as a sister, as a benefactor, and as a Deacon.

There is no authority except the authority of God. Many women in the early church have been enabled through the power of indwelling of the Holy Spirit to perform services that are worthy of God's exultation more than men. Phoebe was a local church leader at the time of the pouring out of the Holy Spirit that was experienced and empowering. This shows that early church Christian women are not regarded as unlearned, or uneducated, or unfit in the service of the Lord.

Phoebe's faith was so strong that she stood with Paul as an ambassador to the believers in Rome. Therefore,

"She *must be* Silent"

Phoebe's life confirmed that early Christian women leaders are officially represented by Christian communities, as well as considerable interest in the society.

It is very interesting that Phoebe is acknowledged as a Deacon in her church; she is also known as Paul's personal representative in the reading and expanding on the letter to the various house churches in Rome. Sometimes, Phoebe might have been the one to interpret or explain the letter to them. Phoebe was the first person that Paul commends in his letter of the list of greetings. This shows that Paul revealed her role as a specific duty to carry Paul's letter to Rome.

This shows believers today the different roles that women did during the early church history. It also appears that Phoebe served in her church in Cenchrea as one of the leaders of her congregation. She was one of the group church leaders, not just traveling minister. Paul wanted the church in Rome to honor Phoebe as a congregational leader by calling Phoebe a sister, which means all Christian are sisters and brothers in Jesus Christ. Phoebe was also known as an official teacher and missionary in the church of Cenchrea and the community.

Phoebe preached to the believers because of her establishment of the house church in her home, which Paul resided during his missionary journey. Phoebe's authority was given by the grace of God as a gift of the Holy Spirit. Her participation in the divine life as a Deacon was a result of her faith in Jesus Christ. The same way Paul exercised authority of his own as an apostle as Bible Scripture recognized and confirmed the spiritual power of Paul and Phoebe. Phoebe's ministry can be seen as full of strength and inspiration of the Holy Spirit.

Today, women must copy Phoebe, teaching and preaching, thereby obtaining what God wants them to be in the church of God instead of following one verse of the Scripture from Paul when he was dealing with the Corinthian women problems. We see here that Paul highly commended and showed his respect to Phoebe in the work of the ministry of our Lord. Paul referred to Phoebe as he referred to Timothy and Titus by calling her Deacon and servant of the church. Apostle Paul said that Phoebe was a benefactor to him, which means that she had helped or supported his missionary journeys financially, and morally means introduced Paul to so many people in Rome. Phoebe served the Lord in a leadership role. Let all the women today follow in her footsteps.

"She *must be* Silent"

One thing I ask of the Lord, this is what I seek: that I may dwell in the house of the Lord all the days of my life, to gaze upon the beauty of the Lord and seek him in his temple."(Psalm 27:4)

CHAPTER FOURTEEN

WHAT BROUGHT OUT CONFUSION IN THE CORINTH CHURCH?

What brought out confusion was the verse in the Corinthian book that contradicted each other. The Corinthian church had so many problems that Paul was trying to straighten out at that time. All the problems connected together, as it started from spiritual gifts of the believer. We have to know that when Paul was dealing with spiritual gifts he did not separate men from women: "The body is a unit, though tit is made up of many parts; and though all its parts are many, they form one body. So it is with Christ. For we were all baptized to one Spirit, into one body –whether Jews or Greeks, slaves, or free –and we were all given the one Spirit to drink" (1st Corinthian 12:12-13). If all we believers of Jesus Christ were baptized by one Spirit which refers to neither water baptism nor to Christ's baptism of the believer in the Holy Spirit, that occurred on the day of Pentecost. Moreover, it rather also refers to the Spirit's baptizing believers into Christ's body, uniting believers in the body and making them spiritually one with other believers.

This is a spiritual transformation of all who gave their life to Jesus Christ. It occurs at the conversion of individuals and puts the believers in Christ. Believers are part of Jesus Christ's body; we are one in Him, as He is one with the Father. Therefore, spiritual gifts should not be the basis for honoring a person either men or women, or considering one believer as more important than another – in the spiritual gifts, men and women are equal in the Lord because we all are one in the Lord. Everyone is placed in Christ's body according to God's will and all members are important for the spiritual well-being and proper functioning of the Body of Christ. We are one in Him and are to serve Him according to our spiritual gift.

"To one there is given through the spirit the message of wisdom, to another the message of knowledge by means of the same spirit, to another faith by the same spirit, to another gifts of healing by that one spirit, to another miraculous power, to another prophecy, to another distinguishing between spirit, to another speaking in different kinds of tongues, and to still another the interpretation of tongues. All these are the work of one and the same spirit, and he gives them to each one, just as he determines (1st Corinthians 12:8-11). The Spirit of God the Father, God the Son and God the Holy Spirit give gifts to all the Body of Christ as He wills. Who is an apostle or a pastor that will say they should be silent and are not to talk. It not a shame for the Holy Spirit to give everyone, including men and women, a spiritual gift for the work of the Lord to strengthen the church for healing and all the services of the Lord.

These spiritual gifts must be used are not to be proud of and are not for individual exaltation, but with a sincere desire to help others and with a heart that genuinely cares for each other and loves the Lord. This is the area in the Book of Corinthians that caused confusion to some people, why the same spirit that gave every man and woman spiritual gifts would turn around and tell some of the part of the body to be silent and not to usurp authority. The authority is the authority of the Holy Spirit that was ordained from Heaven and came down on the Day of Pentecost.

"She *must be* Silent"

This is the reason why people or all the Body of Christ must believe that Apostle Paul was dealing with the problems with the Corinthian church, not the entire church of Christ on Earth. Moreover, how can women be silent in the church? They still have to sing, they still have to pray, and they still have to teach the Scripture. We should all let this clear the confusion: "For God is not a God of disorder, but of peace" (1st Corinthians 14:33).

Even today some men and women still argue in the church and they still have some issues and conflicts between each other, but if every individual has to be silent, how boring will that church be. If they have to be asking their husband at home without going to the Bible study what kind of church would that church be?

Jesus Christ is the Lord of all the people in the world. He said, "Some of the Pharisees in the crowd said to Jesus, 'Teacher, rebuke your disciples!' 'I tell you,' he replied. 'If they keep quiet, the stones will cry out.' " (Luke 19:39-40). If women should be silent in the church, do we want to be replaced with stones? No, Jesus said if the people in the world, meaning men and women, should stop to praise and worship Him, the stones will cry out. It means that all His other created beings and nature will cry out loud and worship Him. How can we read the word of

Jesus Christ in the Scripture and keep silent in the church? How can women use their spiritual gift of the Holy Spirit, if they were to be silent in the church?

Women read the Bible more than some men. Women pray more than some men. Women speak in tongues more than some men. To make it clearer, the same Paul that was telling women in Corinthian's church to be silent, was commending Phoebe in the Cenchrea church for her role as a leader and prophetess. I call on all the women believers of Jesus Christ to know clearly that this verse that caused confusion is only for the Corinthian church women, not all the women in the world. Let us continue to love our Lord and Savior Jesus Christ and let us continue to serve Christians; let us continue to serve Him in the Spirit of holiness.

We all are one body of Christ. Gifts of apostles, prophets, evangelists, pastors, ministers, teachers, gift of miracles, helping others, gift of encouraging others, gift of administration, and gift of leadership: all these spiritual gifts are given to all the Body of Christ as the Spirit sees fit. We should all use all these gifts to enhance the Gospel of God on this Earth before Christ returns.

"She *must be* Silent"

"For in the day of trouble he will keep me safe in his dwelling; he will hide me in the shelter of his tabernacle and set me high upon a rock."(Psalm 27:5)

"She *must be* Silent"

CHAPTER FIFTEEN

CHRIST'S GREAT COMMISSION FOR MEN AND WOMEN BEFORE HIS ASCIENSION

"Then Jesus came to them and said all authority in heaven and on earth has been given to me. Therefore go and make disciples of all nations, baptizing them in the name of the Father and of the Son and of the Holy Spirit, and teaching them to obey everything I have commanded you and surely I am with you always, to the very end of the age." (Matthew 28: 18-20)

Our Lord and Savior Jesus Christ on the day of ascension gave a great commission to all who believed in Him, including those who are going to believe in Him today and forever. When He gave this great commission, He did not say that it is for men only. He gave to men and women five hundred people that were

"She *must be* Silent"

there on that day. The Word of God is God, the same thing continues and it applies to them and applie to us today. Christ is the One and only whom the authority of the Word of God belongs to Christ. Christ gave all those who belong to Him this authority of the Word of God, to go and make disciples of all nations.

If any woman goes to a village and there are men unbelievers, sinners whom Christ died for, is the woman going to say, 'Oh, no, I cannot witness to you because you are a man. I must not use authority over you, or I am a woman you need to wait until a man comes to the village to teach you or preach to you.' Because Paul said a woman must not teach a man? Or the woman says to the man, 'You need a man because women must not usurp authority over men.' What happens if the man died the following day without hearing about Christ?

Christ gave the authority to men and women; there are no distinctions and there is no difference. If any woman preaches, teaches or witnesses, it is the same Word of God, not the word of the woman. If a man preaches or teaches or perhaps healed a sick man, it is the same power of God the Holy Spirit that is doing everything and working through us. The same Word of God through the same Spirit of God by the power of the spiritual gifts of the Holy

Spirit that have been given to every member of the Body of Christ. As long as we are one body of Christ, through the power of the Holy Spirit, we are living for Christ in witnessing, teaching, preaching and doing everything through Christ as believers that are living through Christ. Whatever we do or say in His Holy name, Christ is the one speaking through us, women must use the gift of the Holy Spirit.

The words of Jesus Christ's Great Commission apply to all His followers of every generation, to include men and women. It stated that the goal of believer is to win souls for Christ; it is the responsibility and the commissioning of the Church in mission work and task. We are the Body of Christ; we must go into the entire world and preach and teach the Gospel to all the people in the world. This task includes the primary responsibility of sending missionaries into every village of the Earth.

The preaching of the Gospel which is centered on repentance, forgiveness of sins, surrendering one's life to the Lordship of Jesus Christ, and the promise of receiving the spiritual gift, which the Holy Spirit promised, the exaltation to separate one from this corrupt would, while waiting for Christ returns from Heaven is the believers hope of glory. The main idea is to make disciples: people that will focus on the Lord and give their life wholeheartedly to the Lord. Is there one who will follow Christ commands, which will separate themselves from the world?

Jesus Christ gave the Great Commission and commands all believers', men and women alike, to reach out to the lost men and women of the world. Jesus Christ will be with His obedient servants with the power of the Holy Spirit. All believers', men and women alike, are to go to all the nations and witness the good news to them. Men and women are commissioned to bring the lost to the Savior. If they have to be silent in the Church how could the Great Commission be fulfill through all the believers.

Jesus Christ promised that He would be with all those who believe in Him with His presence and authority. The believers will be witnessing, teaching, preaching and serving the Lord. With that in our mind we have to see clearly that the same Jesus Christ calls all men and women to be in service to Him and commands them to fulfill the Great Commission. All we need to do is to sow the seeds and the Spirit of God will water, and bring out the crops. This command of Jesus Christ of the Great Commission should clear all the Christians women's fears, clear every doubt, every trouble, every heartache and every form of discouragement and confusion that was said to the

"She *must be* Silent"

Corinthian church women by Apostle Paul. We are all one Body of Christ and one in Spirit of Christ.

"She *must be* Silent"

Then my head will be exalted above the enemies who surround me; at his tabernacle will I sacrifice with shouts of joy; I will sing and make music to the Lord." (Psalm 27:6)

CHAPTER SIXTEEN

THE HOLY SPIRIT DECENDED ON THE DAY OF PENTECOST

"When the day of Pentecost came, they were all together in one place; suddenly a sound like the blowing of a violent wind came from heaven and filled the whole house where they were sitting. They saw what seemed to be tongues of fire that separated and came to rest on each of them. All of them were filled with the Holy Spirit and began to speak in other tongues as the spirit enabled them." (Acts 2:1-4)

Another proof of evidence that qualifies men and women to serve the Lord equally is the descending of the Holy Spirit on the Day of Pentecost. On the Day of Pentecost Jesus Christ fulfilled His promise, not only to the apostles, but to everyone that was in Jerusalem and to people from all other nations such as: Parthians, Medes and Elamites, residents of Mesopotamia, Judea and Cappadocia, Pontus and Asia, Phyrgia and Pontus Asia, etc. They heard the apostles in their own language. All these men and women were so perplexed and amazed, but they did not know the meaning. On this particular day was one of the Jewish years. It was a harvest festival when the first fruits of the grain harvest were presented to God. Therefore, God turned this festival day to mark and symbolizes it for the Church the beginning of God's harvest for souls of people in the world.

At the Pentecost event there are three observable manifestations of the Holy Spirit descending upon the people and disciples in fulfillment of the promise of God. There is a rushing winds sound manifestation, like a blowing of a violent wind. The Holy Spirit came down with great power. Wind is one of the scriptural signs for the Holy Spirit. There are also appeared visibly what was like, or looks like a tongue of fire that rested on each of the disciples as a prophetic symbol that the Holy Spirit was coming to empower the apostles and all Christ followers which was a fiery and contagious witnesses for Jesus Christ. On this special day we also have the speech manifestation of the Holy Spirit which fell on men and women both; all the people (one hundred twenty in all) were filled with the Holy Spirit and they began to speak in tongues as the Spirit of God enable them.

The tongue on this special day and on this special occasion was a variety of native languages speaking to other people from different nations that were in the crowd. They spoke all the foreign languages supernaturally and people were surprised and very amazed. God let them know that the witness of the Great Commission is for all the people in the world. The Gospel must be preached, taught and proclaimed by all women and men and to all the men and women in the world. These were the spirit manifestations that came to men and women at the same time with no distinction.

These three observable manifestations on the Day of Pentecost correspond exactly to the promise of the risen Lord to His followers concerning power and witnessing to all the Earth. This shows clearly that our Lord Jesus Christ unmistakably fulfilled His word of promise from His ascended position as our exalted Lord and Jesus Christ at the Father's right hand of authority. All the authority that belongs to Jesus Christ was given to all who believed in Him, both men and women, in the order to take the Gospel to the ends of the Earth.

On the day of Pentecost the Holy Spirit descended from Heaven, and clothed with power from on high, enabling the disciples to witness the resurrection of Jesus Christ and ascension to the people who came from afar and other nations.

They witnessed for Christ and to the people through whom the Holy Spirit could bring great conviction to the lost in relation to sin, righteousness and God's judgment and turn the lost from sin to salvation in Christ. The Holy Spirit revealed by nature as a spirit who longs and strives for salvation of people of every nation.

Those who received the baptism of the Holy Spirit were filled with the same longing for salvation of the human race; therefore, Pentecost is the beginning of the world mission's in that men and women followers of Jesus Christ became ministers of the Spirit. They not only preached Jesus crucified and resurrected, leading others to repentance and faith in Christ, but they also influenced converts to receive the gift of the Holy Spirit whom they themselves had received at Pentecost. This leading others into the baptism in the Holy Spirit is the key to the apostolic work. Through the baptism in the Spirit, Christ's believers are able to become successors to this earthly ministry. They continued to do and to teach in the power of the Holy Spirit, the same things that Jesus began both to do and to teach.

On the day of Pentecost the Spirit of the Lord performed His miracle on men and women in Jerusalem. The Spirit outpouring power was bestowed on both men and women alike. The promise was fulfilled on both men and women. The joy of the Lord that came down from Heaven on that particular day is for men and women. Jesus Christ came into the world to take away our sin, not only for men alone, but for both men and women. The Old Testament of prophetic promises about the coming of Messiah was now fulfilled in Jesus Christ and it marks the beginning and the last. Jesus Christ is both Lord and Christ, crucified Savior, resurrected Lord and exalted redeemer of all the believers of both men and women.

Both men and women must serve Him truthfully and sincerely according to the power of the Holy Spirit who gives gifts to all the Body of Christ, according to ability.

"She *must be* Silent"

"Hear my voice when I call, O Lord; be merciful to me and answer me. My heart says of you, 'Seek his face!' Your face, Lord I will seek."(Psalm 27; 7-8)

CHAPTER SEVENTEEN

HOLY SPIRIT EMPOWERMENT FOR MEN AND WOMEN IN THE CHURCH

What Apostle Paul was saying to the women and men in the Corinthian church is that worship should be in an orderly manner. The church should focus on the Holy Spirit empowerment, which happened then and now suddenly without notice. Worship of the Lord in the power of the Holy Spirit should be centered on comfort, strength, building up the Body of Christ to the glory of God with Spirit empowerment. No one should be arguing or competing in the church and no one should be acting as if they were better than the other, or that they are spiritually higher than the others in the church. Because the Spirit is the one that empowers the individual believer, and the spirit is the one that gives gifts to every believer accordingly as He wills, He can empower one to be an encourager, or the other to be a healer, spiritual preacher or enable one to be preaching with the power of the Holy Spirit and fire. The Spirit can empower another one and bestow the gift of prophecy. The same and one spirit is the one that does and undoes in the life of all the Body of Christ.

The Body of Christ is one, and we are one in Christ Jesus our Lord. These verses: "Women should remain silent in the churches. They are not allowed to speak, but must be in submission as the law says. If they want to inquire about something, they should ask their own husbands at home; for it is disgraceful for a woman to speak in the church" (1st Corinthians 14:34-35). Apostle Paul's spoke these words to the Corinthian Church caused much controversy for many years up until today, making it seem that women are not supposed to serve the Lord, or be participating in the work of the Gospel. This verse has made many women feel useless and they don't want to do anything. They may even look down on any other women who are trying to do something in the Church.

The time is now for women believers of Jesus Christ to serve the Lord in so many ways that the sinners and the lost will be converted to Him. Every minute the Spirit will be able to empower men and women alike for the service of the Lord. All the believers of Jesus Christ should be able to serve the Lord with knowledge and understanding.

There must be an order in the church. No one should envy one another; no one should be speaking in tongues if there is no interpreter. This is what the Spirit is saying to the Churches. Today speaking in tongues still causes controversy. For example, if one is speaking in tongues and the rest of the people in the church were silent and nobody interprets, nobody will know what the Spirit of the Lord is telling the congregation. Moreover, what happens if women are silent in the church, and they decided not to sing in the choir, or on the worship team?

The church will be boring, and there will be no fire of the Holy Spirit. The Spirit power of enabling empowers all the believers to participate in the church and serve the Lord faithfully and truthfully. If we know that all our service for the Lord is through the empowerment of the Holy Spirit, we will not be differentiating that certain work belongs to men, or women, we are limiting ourselves from serving the Lord acceptably. We need to put all our energy, strength, and might focusing on Him who is the author and finisher of our faith and strongly live a life that will bring glory to His Holy name at all times. Everyone must place his or her faith in Jesus Christ as Lord and Savior, repent of their past, present, and future sins in order to be empowered with the Holy Spirit. We are all one in Christ, men and women; we should continue serving Him with the Spirit indwelling power.

"She *must be* Silent"

"Do not hide your face from me, do not turn your servant away in anger; you have been my helper. Do not reject me or forsake me, O God my Savior." (Psalm 27:9)

"She *must be* Silent"

CHAPTER EIGHTEEN

CHRIST CALLED MEN AND WOMEN TO PREACH, TEACH AND TO THE AUTHORITY OF THE WORD

Jesus Christ is the Lord of all people in the world. He was crucified, died and buried and was raised to life for the sins of men and women in this world. Therefore, when He gave the Great Commission, He gave it to both men and women. We also evaluate the doctrine of the Word of God; the Word of God is alive and lives forever. The Word of God is God. We have established that God's words are complete, and sufficient for all who believe in Jesus Christ.

The power of the Holy Spirit was given by God to authenticate revelation, and since then, we have God's complete revelation to men and women; therefore, God's will in the Bible, which made the speaking in tongues unnecessary today. But in those days they didn't have the Word of God as the Bible whereby, individuals can read and understand. God gave His Word to men and women go ye all of you into all the nations and make disciples, teach them all that I have taught you. We have to follow the commands of God if we love Him sincerely. Therefore, when we go out there to witness, preach and teach the Gospel, we are doing it in the power of the Holy Spirit who indwells in us and we are living the life of Christ within us. We have no word of our own and we have no authority of our own, even if we are in the worship service, we still use the Word of God.

We are not alone, and we are doing, saying, teaching, preaching, through the enabling power of the Holy Spirit. The Lord is using the word that He put in our mouth to witness to the sinner and the lost. We are saying what He want us to say. We are to tell them of the way of salvation; Christ is using His authority of the Word through us to witness to the people. Christ uses the Word we gave them to make them alive in Him. Women have the same authority of the Word of God just as the men have the authority of the Word of God.

Jesus continues to call men and women today to serve Him, to make disciples of all nations. There is no

"She *must be* Silent"

doubt in my mind or in my heart, Jesus Christ does not want anyone to be silent in the Church and wants us all to help others that do not know Him, so that they may seek Him and find Him. Men and women must preach, teach and use all the gifts of the Spirit of the Lord for the service of the Lord.

"Though my father and mother forsake me, the Lord will receive me. Teach me your way, O Lord; lead me in a straight path because of my oppressors."(Psalm 27:10-11)

CHAPTER NINETEEN

WOMEN TODAY

Women today must love the Lord with all their heart, soul and body. They must study the Word of God and must be rightly dividing the Word for edification. "Do your best to present yourself to God as one approved a workman who does not need to be ashamed and who correctly handles the word of truth" (2nd Timothy 2:15). Women today should do their best to study at theological schools and biblical training schools that will help women, those who are fervently loyal to God and the Scripture as God's fully inspired Word, making themselves available at all times to the work of the Gospel which Christ entrusted to all the faithful believers. Women must be like soldiers; they must be willing to undergo many difficulties and sufferings and to be ready to wage spiritual warfare in wholehearted devotion to their Lord and Savior.

Women today must work hard like athletes; they must be willing to sacrifice and live a life of strict discipline and be like farmers. They must be patient in seed sowing and committing to hard work and long hours for the service of the Lord. Jesus Christ will carry out His promise for all the believers.

Women today must be ready at all times, in season out of season, in cold weather or hot weather, taking the Gospel of God to the end of the Earth. Women today must make it their number one priority and responsibility to save the lost and the sinners to the holy hands of Jesus Christ.

Women today must be willing to tell others about the love of Jesus Christ to all the people in the world. Women today must enter seminary colleges and Bible colleges, if possible, in order to be ordaining for the work of the Lord.

They must know that Christ gave them the Great Commission on the day of ascension to men and women and we are one in the Body of Christ. Everyone will account for what they have done at the Judgment Seat of Christ to give an account of what they have done to the hopeless sinners who have never had the Gospel preached to them before in their life.

"She *must be* Silent"

"Do not turn me over to the desire of my foes, for false witnesses rise up against me, breathing out violence. I am still confident of this; I will see the goodness of the Lord in the land of the living. Wait for the Lord; be strong and take heart and wait for the Lord." (Psalm 27:12-14)

"She *must be* Silent"

CHAPTER TWENTY

WOMEN ARE EMPOWERED TO PREACH, TEACH AND PRAISE

Christ Jesus did not tell women to be quiet, silent or not to usurp authority over men. We have to know that those words are just Paul's words. God's Word must be received, believed and obeyed as the final authority in all things pertaining to life and godliness. Jesus Christ loved men and women and the power of the Holy Spirit is given to both men and women to serve the Lord. We must all give an account of things we have done for Christ after we have been saved.

Women are empowered to preach, teach, pray and praise the Lord in everything they are going through in their lives. We must preach to our children, our husband, our friends, and our neighbors, our co-workers, so that if they don't know the Lord or have never heard about the

Gospel of God that they would find salvation. Women must show the people of this world the way of salvation of Jesus Christ.

We must know that Christ died and rose for all the believers, not for men alone; He gave us the Great Commission as He gave it to women. We must be a good steward of the Word of God, praying without ceasing, preaching, teaching, praising the Lord in every situation, in every season, in every problem, in every conflict and in every adversity. This is what will enrich the lives of men and women, helping them to grow in the Lord.

Women must study to know what the Lord was saying in every Scripture verse. Women must be vigilant, courageous, and understand the will of the Lord for their lives and the lives of their children. Women must use God's Word, given by the Holy Spirit, as our full and sufficient guide which to judge what we believe and do. Women must follow the Scriptural teaching of the Word of God: "Therefore, I urge you brothers, in view of God's mercy to offer your bodies as living sacrifices, holy and pleasing to God this is your spiritual act of worship" (Romans 12:1).

Christian women and because of God's profound mercy to us in Christ, should be willingly to offer their bodies to God as living sacrifices for His honor, praise and glory. Women believers' greatest desire should be to live lives of holy worship and devotion to God. This means we must separate ourselves from the pattern of this world. Believers must pursue God in holy passion and focus on the Lord. Our bodies are to be consecrated to God for a lifetime of worship and service. We are to offer our bodies as dead to sin, instruments of righteousness and as the temple of the Holy Spirit that indwells us.

"She *must be* Silent"

"Come, all Christians be committed to the service of the Lord; make your lives for him more fitted, turn your hearts with one accord. Come into his courts with gladness, all your sacred vows renew, turn away from sin and sadness, be transformed with life a new." (Words of Eve B. Lloyed, 1966)

SUMMARY

The great doctrine revealed in the Scripture are redemptive truth: Christ called men and women to serve Him without distinction. Christ is the Lord of all. He came to this world to save sinners of which I am one of them. Christ is our Redeemer King, in Him there is life, life everlasting.

There is a proof, without reasonable doubt, that shows that Apostle Paul was dealing and directing His word to the women in the Corinthian church who were causing confusion and that did not want anyone else to talk in the church. As a form of discipline, Paul told them to be silent. Early church men used this verse to take advantage of women in the world, and to oppress them to the point that they even became silent in the Church.

When we look at it, the same Paul was commending a woman for a good work as a prophetess and as a leader. Even today some women still caused arguments, or wanted to use certain words that are not appropriate in the Church. With this in mind, we have to know that Jesus Christ calls men and women to take the Gospel of God to the end of the Earth. Beginning from the Old Testament to the New Testament, women served the Lord in a mighty way and they held leadership roles, which brought glory to the Lord.

Jesus Christ is the same yesterday, today and tomorrow; let us serve the Lord with the Spirit of holiness; let us use the gift of the Spirit of God to serve Him by doing what is going to bring sinners and the lost to His Holy hands. We women today must make haste. Our Lord is waiting to hear from us and to see us women bring the people of the world to His feet for salvation in Christ as our salvation is completed. Hallelujah. Let us rejoice in the Lord our Redeemer King who brought immortality in the light.

"She *must be* Silent"

"Of your time and talents give ye, they are gifts from God above, to be used by Christians freely to proclaim his wondrous love. Come again to serve the Savior, tithes and offerings with you bring; in your work, with him find favor, and with joy his praises sing."(Words of Eve Be. Lloyed, 1966)

"She *must be* Silent"

PRAYER

Lord Jesus Christ, our Lord and Savior, I pray that you perform your miracle in the lives of the women believers and non-believers that are still going to hear the Gospel preached to them, or the Gospel of God taught to them in seminary schools, Bible colleges or Bible training schools all over the Earth. Help them and energize their spirit, soul, and body to take the Gospel of God to the end of the Earth. Let them be able to focus on Thee and be active in all the areas of service in the work of the Lord.

The Scripture said: "Then he said to his disciples. The harvest is plentiful but the workers are few. Ask the Lord of the harvest, therefore, to send out workers into his harvest field." (Matthew 9:37-38) Help them through the power of your indwelling of the Holy Spirit to live a life of a soul winner, a life of holiness, bringing sinners to you throughout every minute and every second of their days on Earth. You do not want anyone to perish; help women in

"She *must be* Silent"

this world to reach the unreachable for you. Let the women make it a priority and duty to witness to men and women sinners and the lost and unbelievers, people of all other religions, and the atheist who believe there is no God. Let your full presence be known in the lives of all the women on Earth who preach and teach with the Spirit empowerment through them. Release them from all the oppressions, rejections, persecutions and violent behaviors that some of them might be going through in the hands of men around the world. Look down from Heaven, stretch your Holy hands and move them up, so that they can do great things in the work of the Gospel of God that will exalt Your Holy Name.

You are God the Creator of men and women. In Your loving kindness, move women in this Earth from the bondage of oppression, so that they can be useful, and give their entire life to you, instead of giving their life to men. You are the God of all creations; You created men and women for Your great glory. In Your infinite love help all the women on this Earth to know you and shed your love unto their hearts, so that they can be able to love you more and more, and surrender all into your Lordship. In your matchless Holy Name, the Name above all names, I pray, accept my prayers. Amen.

"She *must be* Silent"

"Come in praise and adoration, all who on Christ's name believe; worship him with consecration, grace and love will you receive. For this grace give him the glory, for the Spirit and the Word, and repeat the gospel story until all his name have heard." (Words of Eve B. Lloyd, 1966)

"She *must be* Silent"

BIBLIOGRAPHY

Evangelical Dictionary of Biblical Theology, Edited by Walter A. Elwell, Baker Books, A Division of Baker Book House Company, Grand Rapids, Michigan (1996).

Henry, Matthew, Commentary on the Whole Bible, Edited by Rev. Leslie F. Church, Ph.D., F. R. Hist. S., Zondervan Publishing House, Grand Rapids, Michigan (1960).

MacDonald, William, Believer's Bible Commentary: A Complete Bible Commentary In One Volume, Edited by Art Farstad, Thomas Nelson Publishers, Nashville (1980).

Smart, James D., The Interpretation of Scripture, The Westminster Press, Philadelphia, USA.

Thomas F. Torrance, Paul D. Molnar, Theologian of the Trinity: Christian Denominations Doctrine Theology the Bible, Ashgate Publisher, Ltd: Distributed by Syndetic Solutions, Inc., Theologian of the Trinity: Christian Denominations Doctrine Theology the Bible. Farnham, England. Burlington, VT (1946).

BIBLICAL INDEX

Genesis 1:26, 1:27, 21:14-19

Exodus 15:20, 33:15, 2:1-10

2nd Chronicles 34:22-26

Judges 4:4-6

Ezra 2:64-65

Joel 2:28-29

Esther 4:14

Matthew 16:21-23, 28:18-20, 9:37

Luke 2:21-28, 2:36-38, 19:39-40

John 4:7-9, 4:16, 4:28-30, 4:39-42, 10:38-42, 20:17

Acts: 18:26, 18:18, 24-26, 18:26, 2:1-4

Romans 16:1-2, 13:1-2, 12:1

1st Corinthians 7:32-33, 2:12, 14:29-31, 14:33-35, 12:12-13, 12:8-11, 14:33

Galatians 2: 11-14

1st Timothy 2:12

2nd Timothy 2:15

"She *must be* Silent"

Books previously Published by the author:
Grace Dola Balogun
by
Grace Religious Books Publishing & Distributors, Inc.
New York

"She *must be* Silent"

PRAYER THE SOURCE OF STRENGTH FOR LIFE - English Edition

Prayer the Source of Strength for Life is a powerful book that will energize your spirit to pray more and more until the prayer is part of your life and until the gate of Heaven is opened and your prayer is answered. Your prayer life will change your life.

LA ORACION FUENTE DE FORTALEZA PARA LA VIDA – Spanish Edition.

Dios no's dio el poder de la oracion, quiere que lo usemos; debemos illamar, comunicarnos con el en todo lo que estemo spasando. El espera saber denosotros.

Spirit Power Volumes I and II

Spirit Power Volumes I and II both discuss the power of the Holy Spirit in the lives of believers.

The Power of the Spirit of God begins from the creation of the world up until today. That power will also continue until Christ returns to reign. Hallelujah

"She *must be* Silent"

THE CROSS AND THE CRUCIFIXION

Our Lord Jesus Christ died on the Cross to bring forth love and compassion. Sin's impact on human life brings all other evil into our world, from one society to another society, from one culture to another.

But in Christ, we are clothed with His holiness. We have the gift of eternal life. The gate of Heaven is open and we are eligible for our inheritance in Heaven.

Hallelujah! Hosanna in the Highest. Jesus Christ paid it all, unto Him all we owe. The Cross of Christ is the Cross of joy, peace, and righteousness to all who believe in Him.

Three Simple Solutions for World Peace

Three Simple Solutions for World Peace is a book that clears all the confusion that many people of the world have been going through for many years. It is a book that gives light and advice to some of the problems that plague the world, and that offers solutions for these problems. It is a book that is full of knowledge, understanding and solutions that will bring some peace to the world.

JUSTIFICATION BY FAITH ALONE IN CHRIST ALONE

Grace Dola Balogun

Justification by Faith Alone in Christ Alone

Justification by Faith Alone in Christ Alone will clear all the confusion of believers' faith in Jesus Christ. Believers will also rejoice in the long sufferings – they will rejoice in their sufferings, afflictions, persecutions, rejections and all various trials that may press in on them because these long-sufferings will help all the believers to be redeemed in Christ.

CHRISTIAN CELL PHONE SERIES:

Christian Cell Phone Godly Wisdom helps readers understand the role of God's wisdom and the importance of obtaining godly wisdom in one's life to produce prosperous results in all areas of life. These areas are critical and include family, relationships and finances. The acquiring of God's wisdom is to be sought after in life and will impact others as well.

Christian Cell Phone God's Favor is designed to give readers knowledge of God's favor from the Old Testament to the New Testament. With an analysis of the favor that was on Jesus, the Son of God, the reader will find that God's favor can completely change one's life and lead others to Christ as well.

Christian Cell Phone God's Anointing takes a look at the anointing on the life of Jesus that includes present day believers in Christ Jesus. This anointing can be applied to all areas of life and can be seen in miraculous ways. The anointing is what makes our life incredible and supernatural, drawing all those who see, to Christ.

JESUS CHRIST THE JOY OF CHRISTMAS

Jesus Christ the Joy of Christmas gives praise and tribute to the child that was born in Bethlehem. Tracing the prophecies of Old about this King that was born, the author gives an account of the sinless Lamb of God who came to take away the peoples' sin from a biblical perspective, who is the real Joy of Christmas.

PRAYER FOR THE BULLY VICTIMS AND THE BULLY TOO!

Prayer for the Bully Victims and the Bully Too addresses the issue of the bully from the classroom to the home. By the use of scriptural application, the author takes a look at what can be done to help the bully kid and their victims. The author has written several key prayers that readers can use to help either the bully victim or parents who are dealing with a child that has become a bully.

I AM THE RESURRECTION AND THE LIFE

I Am The Resurrection and The Life: Powerful, inspirational and written from a firm biblical perspective, multi-published author Grace Dola Balogun, gives life to others through the power of Jesus Christ who is the Resurrection and the life. This book will open eyes to the amazing and abundant blessings of accepting Jesus Christ as your Lord and Savior, giving keen insight into the Scriptures on the power available to all through the Holy Spirit with an emphasis on aspects of eternal life for the believer.

I AM THE ETERNAL LIFE

I Am The Eternal Life: Encouraging, uplifting and filled with a sound biblical perspective, this book encourages believers and non-believers alike to look to the One that is Jesus Christ, the Son of God, who is the Bread of life and the one who gives eternal life to all who believe in Him. This book gives readers a heavenly perspective on their life, revealing believer's God-given destiny and purpose to all who call on Jesus Christ as their Lord and Savior. The truth of the Gospel and the Good News is eloquently displayed in this delightful and insightful read.

HE WHO BELIEVES IN ME SHALL NEVER DIE

He Who Believes In Me Shall Never is a fascinating teaching, revealing Jesus as the way, the truth and the life - the Everlasting life. All who believe in Him shall never die. Beginning from the Old Testament, the author takes a look at the fall of humanity through the sin of disobedience through Adam and Eve. Comparing this fall to the sin of disobedience today, the author reveals scriptural truths in the lives of Enoch, Elijah and Moses. The author gives insight into the baptism of the Holy Spirit and gives examples of the Spirit's power and the purpose for which the power is given to believers. The author has given key scriptural insights that all who believe in Jesus Christ will have everlasting life in Him that continues to Heaven.

FORGIVE OUR DEBTS AS WE FORGIVE OUR DEBTORS

Forgive Our Debts As We Forgive Our Debtors speaks of divine forgiveness from the Lord and the Lord's commandment to forgive others, including ourselves. With the Lord's Prayer as a foundation, author Grace D. Balogun, explores from the Old Testament to the New Testament meanings of forgiveness and the consequences of sin. The author gives keen biblical insight into the subject of forgiveness, bringing life-changing healing that is only acquired through the power of forgiveness.

ABOUT THE AUTHOR

Grace Dola Balogun graduated from Fordham University Graduate School of Religion and Religious Education in the year 2010 with an M.A. in Religion and Religious Education. She has been a prayer mentor and advisor for many Christians of all denominations for many years.

Visit her online at:
www.Gracereligiousbookspublishers.com
Facebook
Twitter @prayersource

To order additional copies of this book, please E-mail: info@gracereligiousbookspublishers.com.

This book may also be ordered from 30,000 wholesalers, retailers, and booksellers in the U. S., and in Canada and over 100 countries globally.

To contact Grace Dola Balogun for an interview or a speaking engagement, please E-mail:

info@gracereligiousbookspublishers.com

"She *must be* Silent"

The Spirit and the bride say,
"Come!" And let the one who hears say, "Come!" Let the
one who is thirsty come;
and let the one who wishes take the free
gift of the water of life (Revelation 22:17).

MARANATHA EVEN SO COME LORD JESUS (1ST CORINTHIANS 16:22, REVELATION 22:20)

ORDER FORM

TO ORDER YOUR COPY OF ANY BOOK:

NAME:_____
ADDRESS:_____
_____
TELEPHONE:_____
FAX#:_____
MAIL:_____
QUANTITY:_____

MAIL TO:

Grace Religious Books Publishing & Distributors, Inc.
New York
213 Bennett Avenue
              New York, NY 10040

"She *must be* Silent"

www.ingramcontent.com/pod-product-compliance
Lightning Source LLC
Chambersburg PA
CBHW030327080526
44584CB00012B/743